CELEBRATING OUR HOLIDAYS

Celebrating VETERANS DAY

By Elizabeth Morgan and
Elaine Landau

Cavendish Square
New York

Published in 2023 by Cavendish Square Publishing, LLC
29 E. 21st Street New York, NY 10010

Website: cavendishsq.com

Library of Congress Cataloging-in-Publication Data

Names: Morgan, Elizabeth, 1993- author. | Landau, Elaine. Veterans Day–remembering our war heroes.
Title: Celebrating Veterans Day / Elizabeth Morgan, Elaine Landau.
Description: New York : Cavendish Square Publishing, [2023] | Series: Celebrating our holidays | Includes index.
Identifiers: LCCN 2021042157 | ISBN 9781502664891 (set) | ISBN 9781502664907 (library binding) | ISBN 9781502664884 (paperback) | ISBN 9781502664914 (ebook)
Subjects: LCSH: Veterans Day–Juvenile literature.
Classification: LCC D671 .M675 2023 | DDC 394.264–dc23
LC record available at https://lccn.loc.gov/2021042157

Editor: Katie Kawa
Copyeditor: Jill Keppeler
Designer: Deanna Paternostro

The photographs in this book are used by permission and through the courtesy of: Cover, p. 1 cvm/Shutterstock.com; back cover, pp. 3, 5, 7, 9, 11, 15, 16, 21, 23, 25, 28, 29, 30, 31, 32 N.D.Vector/Shutterstock.com; p. 4 Anthony Correia/Shutterstock.com; pp. 6, 26 Getmilitaryphotos/Shutterstock.com; pp. 8, 10 Everett Collection/Shutterstock.com; pp. 12–13, 22 Pamela Au/Shutterstock.com; p. 14 Juneisy Q. Hawkins/Shutterstock.com; p. 16 Donna Beeler/Shutterstock.com; pp. 18–19 Zack Frank/Shutterstock.com; p. 20 Evgeniy Kalinovskiy/Shutterstock.com; p. 23 TJ Brown/Shutterstock.com; p. 24 Eduard Moldoveanu/Shutterstock.com; p. 27 1000Photography/Shutterstock.com; p. 28 Olya Detry/Shutterstock.com.

CPSIA compliance information: Batch #CSCSQ23: For further information contact Cavendish Square Publishing LLC, New York, New York, at 1-877-980-4450.

Printed in the United States of America

CONTENTS

Veterans Day is a day to honor those who've served in the U.S. military. Do you know anyone who's a veteran?

CHAPTER ONE

Who Are Veterans?

Every year on November 11, citizens of the United States celebrate Veterans Day. This is a day set aside to honor veterans—people who've served in the military. Some veterans fought in wars, while others served their country during times of peace. Veterans Day celebrates all of these brave people. It's important to learn about what veterans have done for their country so you can better understand why this day is so special.

The Branches of the Military

In the United States, veterans are people who were once part of the U.S. military, or armed forces. The U.S. military is divided into six main branches. Veterans Day honors people who've served in any of these branches.

The U.S. Air Force deals with protecting people and fighting wars from the sky. The U.S. Army fights battles on the ground. Both the U.S. Coast Guard and U.S. Navy protect waterways. The Coast Guard works closer to the U.S. mainland, and the U.S. Navy protects waters that go beyond the Coast Guard's reach. The U.S. Marine Corps supports other branches and

Shown here are members of the U.S. Army.

Reserves and the National Guard

Some veterans served their country as active-duty members of the military. This means they were full-time members of their branch of the military. Veterans who served in the reserves of their military branches, however, didn't serve full-time. Members of the reserves are trained but called to serve only when needed. In addition, members of the National Guard also serve when needed, especially in their state. They often help after natural **disasters** or other **emergencies.**

fights on land, in the air, and at sea. The U.S. Space Force is part of the Air Force and deals with space.

Not an Easy Life

Veterans—both those who fought in wars and those who served during peacetime—didn't have an easy job. People who serve in the military often have to spend long periods of time away from home. They don't get to see their loved ones very often. In some cases, they're put in very dangerous, or unsafe, situations. This can be very hard for their **mental** health. In some cases, they can get hurt too. It can take a lot of time and hard work for them to get better.

Veterans Day is a good day to take a closer look at how veterans are treated in the United States. Many people believe the health-care services, jobs, and other kinds of help offered to veterans need to be better. Veterans can sometimes feel like their hard work protecting their country has gone unnoticed or unappreciated. That's why this holiday is so important. It's a chance to thank the people who've served our country for all they've done for us.

Veterans Day is celebrated on November 11, which is the day fighting stopped at the end of World War I in 1918. That war was called "the war to end all wars," although we know now that wasn't true.

CHAPTER TWO

THE HISTORY OF THE HOLIDAY

Veterans Day is a federal holiday—a day when the entire United States celebrates a holiday and government offices, banks, schools, and many businesses are closed. Although there have been veterans in the United States since after the time of the American Revolution (1775–1783), Veterans Day hasn't always been a federal holiday in this country. However, things began to change after World War I ended in 1918.

THE IMPORTANCE OF NOVEMBER 11

World War I began in 1914. The causes of this war were **complex**. A number of nations had become enemies. Each wanted to be the most powerful. They built strong armies and navies and formed **alliances** to protect themselves. When Archduke Franz Ferdinand of Austria-Hungary was assassinated, or killed, the **tensions** between these nations exploded into war.

Most of the fighting in World War I took place in Europe, but it was a war that **involved** countries around the world, including the United States. About 10 million soldiers from both sides were killed, and at least 20 million more were wounded, or hurt.

Early on November 11, 1918, the countries fighting the war agreed to make peace. At 11 a.m. that day, the fighting stopped. Soldiers on battlefields put down their guns. The good news spread. Businesses closed so workers could celebrate this happy day and honor those who didn't live to see it.

The Anniversary of the Armistice

The soldiers who fought in World War I weren't forgotten. On November 11, 1919, President Woodrow Wilson declared the day Armistice Day in the United States. "Armistice" means the end of

Many countries fought in World War I, so many countries began honoring Armistice Day in 1919.

November 11 Around the World

November 11 is an important day in many countries outside the United States too. In Australia, Canada, and some other countries, the day is known as Remembrance Day. The United Kingdom also celebrates Remembrance Day, as well as Remembrance Sunday, which is held on the second Sunday of November. In France and Belgium, November 11 is still known as Armistice Day. Special services, parades, and other events are held around the world to honor veterans on this day.

fighting in a war. Armistice Day was held on the **anniversary** of the end of World War I and served as a day to honor the war's veterans.

People in the United States wanted Armistice Day to be an official holiday. People wrote to their lawmakers to ask them to help. In 1926, lawmakers officially asked the president to mark every November 11 as a holiday. Twelve years later, in 1938, U.S. lawmakers and made Armistice Day a federal holiday. This was still a holiday to honor the veterans of World War I. It would take another world war to lead to the holiday of Veterans Day as we know it today.

Beyond World War I

The end of World War I didn't mean the end of all wars. In fact, the way the end of that war was handled created problems that led to the next world war. In 1939, World War II began. The United States entered this war in 1941. Millions of soldiers died or were wounded in this war before it ended in 1945.

Today's Veterans Day celebrations honor all veterans—not just those who served in World War I.

Only five years after World War II ended, the Korean War began. Americans also fought and died in this war, which lasted until 1953. After World War II and the Korean War, many Americans thought there should be a holiday to honor all veterans, not just those who had fought in World War I. Once again, they asked their leaders for help. In 1954, President Dwight D. Eisenhower signed an important bill into law. November 11 became known as Veterans Day to recognize the importance of all veterans.

Today, Veterans Day recognizes veterans who fought in these wars, as well as the Vietnam War (1954–1975), the Persian Gulf War (1990–1991), the War in Afghanistan (2001–2021), and the Iraq War (2003–2011). It also honors military members who didn't fight in wars but still served their country.

The World War II Memorial in Washington, D.C., was built to honor the Americans who served in this war. Special events are held there every year on Veterans Day, and similar Veterans Day events are held at other memorials around the country.

CHAPTER THREE
HONORING VETERANS

There are many ways Americans celebrate Veterans Day. Many people take time to thank the veterans they know. There are also many public events held to thank veterans in communities across the country. These events show the people who served their country in the military that their fellow Americans value their service.

SPECIAL GROUPS AND SPECIAL CEREMONIES

Many communities have special groups for veterans. These groups often plan Veterans Day ceremonies, or events to honor a certain anniversary or other special day. One example of this kind of group is the Veterans of Foreign Wars (VFW). The American Legion is another veterans group. These groups allow veterans to come together for friendship, support, and activities, including Veterans Day activities.

The ceremonies these groups plan sometimes take place at military **cemeteries** or parts of other cemeteries where veterans are buried. Other times, they take place in front of memorials or monuments in communities that honor veterans. Government leaders sometimes speak at these ceremonies, and current members of the military are often there too.

The POW/MIA Flag

POW/MIA flags can sometimes be seen at Veterans Day ceremonies and other events. POW stands for "prisoner of war." These are soldiers who were taken prisoner by the enemy. MIA stands for "missing in action." These are soldiers who were lost in battle. No one knows what happened to them. They might have been taken prisoner, or they might have been killed. Their bodies were never found. POW/MIA flags remind us not to forget these soldiers when we honor veterans.

The POW/MIA flag has an important message written on it: "You are not forgotten." It reminds us that all veterans are remembered on November 11.

Other people often come to these ceremonies to support family members who are veterans or simply to thank the veterans in their community. Veterans are often asked to stand so people can clap and cheer for them to show their thanks.

The Tomb of the Unknown Soldier

One of the most important Veterans Day ceremonies in the United States takes place at the **Tomb** of the Unknown Soldier in Arlington National Cemetery. It faces the Potomac River and Washington, D.C. The body of a soldier who died in World War I was placed in the tomb on November 11, 1921. No one knows his name, and his body couldn't be identified.

In 1958, two more soldiers were buried there. One had died in World War II. The other was killed in the Korean War. In 1984, a fourth soldier was also buried there. He died in the Vietnam War. However, his identity was later discovered. His body was then given to his family, so they could bury him according to their wishes. As of 2021, there are three soldiers buried in this tomb. They represent, or stand for, all the unknown soldiers who died in wars and were never given a proper burial by their loved ones.

Each year on Veterans Day, a ceremony is held at the Tomb of the Unknown Soldier. It always takes place on November 11 at exactly 11 a.m. The time and date are important. World War I stopped at 11 a.m. on November 11, 1918. That was the 11th hour of the 11th day of the 11th month.

All the different military branches take part in the ceremony. There are two minutes of silence. No one speaks during that time out of respect for the dead soldiers.

A wreath is placed at the tomb by the president of the United States or someone chosen to represent them. A military bugle song called "Taps" is played. Everyone stands quietly. This is a sad but important

Visitors to Arlington National Cemetery can see the Tomb of the Unknown Soldier any day, but Veterans Day is a special time to visit this important monument.

ceremony. A similar one is held on Memorial Day, which is a day set aside to honor the people who've died serving their country in the military.

Why Wear a Flower?

Some people wear a special flower on Veterans Day. The flowers are called poppies. Artificial, or man-made, Buddy Poppies are sold by members of the VFW. Veterans make these red flowers that people pin to their clothing. The money made by selling these flowers is then used to help veterans across the United States as well as children who need help. The American Legion also makes and sells poppies to raise money for veterans.

The poppy has a special meaning. It plays a big part in a poem called "In Flanders Fields," which was written by a Canadian soldier in World War I named John McCrae. The soldier was a doctor who treated many dying men, yet all around the graves, poppies grew. His famous poem is written from the point of view of the soldiers who lost their lives in battle. They ask readers not to forget what they fought for. Today, people in the United States and in many other countries wear poppies on and around November 11 to show that they haven't forgotten the soldiers McCrae wrote about.

Many kids have family members who are veterans. Veterans Day is a special day for them to celebrate the people in their lives who served their country in the military.

CHAPTER FOUR

WHAT CAN KIDS DO?

Veterans Day is celebrated by people across the United States, and this means kids can take part in the celebrations too. From attending parades and ceremonies to making cards to say thank you to veterans, there are many ways kids can celebrate Veterans Day—both in school and in their community.

ATTENDING A PARADE

Many communities have their own Veterans Day parades. Because kids are off from school on this holiday, they can attend one of these parades with their family. Veterans often march in the parades, and government leaders sometimes do too. Some Veterans Day parades feature school marching bands playing patriotic songs, or songs that show pride in the United States. They might have patriotic floats too.

In addition, people often carry flags down the parade route. These flags include the U.S. flag, the flags of the different military branches, and the POW/MIA flag. Kids who are watching the parade may be given small American flags to wave.

It's been said that the biggest Veterans Day parade in the world takes place in New York City. It started in 1919, which makes it the oldest Veterans Day parade in the country. In 1919, it was actually held in September to welcome home soldiers who'd served in

Communities of all sizes host Veterans Day parades. Some parades, such as the one in New York City, are very large, while others are much smaller but still filled with pride and patriotism.

World War I. Today, more than 25,000 people march in the parade down Fifth Avenue.

Learning About Veterans

Although schools are closed on Veterans Day, many students spend the days around the holiday learning about veterans. This can include reading books or watching movies about veterans and the wars they fought in. It can also include getting a visit from a veteran.

Some schools have Veterans Day presentations in which a veteran speaks to students about their experiences. This veteran might be a family member of a student or someone from the surrounding community. Students are able to ask questions about life in the military and get honest answers from someone who knows best. They're also able to thank a veteran in person for their service.

Making Cards and Other Ways to Celebrate

One of the most popular ways students prepare for Veterans Day in school is by making cards to send to veterans, especially those in hospitals. These cards are often decorated with American flags that students draw themselves. Inside, students write messages thanking a veteran for their service to their country. These cards can help make a veteran's day brighter, and they're fun for students to make too.

In many schools, students also write about Veterans Day. They might write about why this holiday is important, the history of the holiday, or someone they know who's a veteran. Some schools ask students to talk to a veteran in their community and share their story.

Handmade signs thanking veterans are a common sight in communities and schools across the United States every November.

School and community libraries often put out books about wars and soldiers on Veterans Day. Kids and adults can check out these books to learn even more about the people honored on this holiday. Businesses and families across the United States put out the American flag on this special day to show their support for the people who've protected this country over the years. It often makes veterans feel good to see this support, and there are many ways Americans can keep showing it far beyond November 11.

MILITARY FAMILIES

Veterans Day is an important day to think about the sacrifices made not only by veterans themselves but also by their family members. Being in a military family can be hard. Military families often move around a lot, so kids whose parents are in the military may go to many different schools. They're also sometimes separated from their loved one who's in the military for long periods of time. If you know someone who's part of a military family, Veterans Day is a good day to let them know you care about them too.

The Empire State Building in New York City is often lit up in patriotic colors on holidays such as Veterans Day. This day is important, but it's also important not to forget about veterans when it's over.

CHAPTER FIVE

BEYOND VETERANS DAY

Veterans Day is a special holiday that reminds Americans not only of the important things veterans have done for their country but also of the issues and problems they often face in the years after their service has ended. Veterans sometimes struggle to **adjust** to life as civilians, or people who aren't actively serving in the military. They can feel lonely. This is why it's important to make veterans feel supported far beyond Veterans Day.

MENTAL HEALTH MATTERS

Some veterans deal with wounds and other physical, or bodily, problems that are easy to see after they return from serving their country. They might be missing an arm or a leg, or they might use a wheelchair to get around.

These veterans and many others also often deal with pain that's not as easy to see. They might have lost friends in a battle, struggled with loneliness, or felt lost when they returned home and had to adjust to life away from the military. These and many other experiences can lead to mental health conditions that hurt veterans just as much as problems with their physical health.

Veterans often have to deal with scary, sad, and lonely times while they're serving their country. It's often good for them to find someone they trust to talk to about these hard times.

Veterans sometimes have a hard time talking about their mental health or asking for help when they feel bad. They might also have a hard time getting help when they need it because there can be long waits to get help at veterans' health centers.

Mental health struggles can even cause some veterans to lose their homes. Homelessness is a big problem among veterans, and as many as 40,000 veterans might be homeless on any given night in the United States.

SHOWING SUPPORT

Veterans Day is often seen as a happy day of giving thanks, so it can be sad to learn about the problems veterans face. However, there are many things that can be done to help veterans in your community on Veterans Day and beyond.

One of the most important things you can do is offer support to veterans you know. You can also encourage veterans you know to join support groups with other veterans. These groups often help veterans feel less alone.

Dealing with PTSD

Fighting in a war can make many veterans feel on edge long after they're home and the danger has passed. This is a common sign of a mental health condition called post-traumatic stress disorder (PTSD). Other signs of PTSD can include problems with sleeping and having bad dreams. PTSD is a serious problem, so it's important for a veteran who thinks they might be dealing with it to get help.

Raising money for groups that help veterans is another way people can help. In addition, you can write to government leaders about veterans' issues and ask these leaders to give more support to veterans. Even the simple act of making a card for a veteran in the hospital can make a big difference. This common Veterans Day craft can be a special activity at any other time of the year too.

The feelings of pride and gratitude we feel on November 11 shouldn't go away when that day ends. The spirit of Veterans Day should last the whole year.

Thanking veterans for their service is a common Veterans Day activity, but it's important to make veterans feel appreciated on more than just one day.

HOLIDAY HOW-TO

Make a Poppy Wreath

You Will Need:

strong paper plate
ruler
pencil
black marker
paint and paintbrush (colors: green, red, and black)
scissors
egg carton
glue

You can hang this poppy wreath in your house on Veterans Day or give it to a veteran you know as a gift!

Directions:

1. Use a ruler to draw two horizontal lines (going left to right) across the middle of the paper plate, with about 1.5 inches (3.8 centimeters) between them.
2. Cut out the two inner half circles from the paper plate, leaving the horizontal line and the outside rim, or the outer edge (so it looks like a wreath with a line across the middle).
3. Write "Remember" in the middle of the wreath.
4. Paint everything but the middle line on the plate green. Let it dry.
5. While the plate is drying, cut the individual cups out of the egg carton.
6. Cut into each egg carton cup in two places but not all the way to the base. With the break in the cup from where it touched the carton, your cups should look like they each have three petals.
7. Push the petals back slightly. (You might need to round the edges of the cups to make them look more like flowers. You can ask an adult for help cutting the edges!)
8. Paint each cup red. Let them dry.
9. Paint the center of each cup black. Let them dry again.
10. Glue the poppy flowers you made on the wreath.

GLOSSARY

adjust: To become used to a new way of doing things.

alliance: A group of people or countries joined together in some activity or effort.

anniversary: A date that is remembered or celebrated because a special event happened on that date in a previous year.

cemetery: A place where dead people are buried.

complex: Not easy to understand or explain.

disaster: Something that happens suddenly and causes much suffering and loss for many people.

emergency: An unexpected and often unsafe situation that calls for immediate action.

involve: To include as a part of.

memorial: Something created to honor a person who has died.

mental: Relating to the mind.

tension: A state in which people, groups, or countries disagree with and feel anger toward each other.

tomb: A building or chamber above or below the ground in which a dead body is kept.

FIND OUT MORE

Books

Friesen, Helen Lepp. *Veterans Day*. New York, NY: Smartbook Media Inc., 2021.

Houser, Grace. *Why Do We Celebrate Veterans Day?* New York, NY: PowerKids Press, 2019.

Jones, Emma. *Who Are Veterans?* New York, NY: KidHaven Publishing, 2020.

Websites

Arlington National Cemetery
www.arlingtoncemetery.mil/#!/
Visit this website to learn more about the Tomb of the Unknown Soldier and to plan a trip to this important place to honor veterans.

5 Facts to Know About Veterans Day
www.defense.gov/Explore/Features/story/Article/1675470/5-facts-to-know-about-veterans-day/
This U.S. government website lists important facts about Veterans Day and has a link to a quiz you can take to test your knowledge of this holiday.

Publisher's note to educators and parents: Our editors have carefully reviewed these websites to ensure that they are suitable for students. Many websites change frequently, however, and we cannot guarantee that a site's future contents will continue to meet our high standards of quality and educational value. Be advised that students should be closely supervised whenever they access the Internet.

INDEX